What is about 4 feet tall,
with Blond hair
likes Yogurt + Ramen
(see Back Page For Answer

Merry christmas
Love — Dad
&
Cristy

GIANTS!

A RIDDLE BOOK
and

Mr. Bigperson's Side
A Story Book

GIANTS!

A RIDDLE BOOK

and

Mr. Bigperson's Side

A Story Book

By Jane Sarnoff and Reynold Ruffins

Charles Scribner's Sons, New York

To our big brothers

Library of Congress Cataloging in Publication Data
Sarnoff, Jane.
Giants! A riddle book and Mr. Bigperson's side: A story book
SUMMARY: A collection of riddles and a story about giants.
1. Riddles—Juvenile literature. (1. Riddles. 2. Giants—Fiction) I. Ruffins, Reynold. II. Title.
PN6371.5.S285   398.6   77-6727   ISBN 0-684-15196-0

1 3 5 7 9 11 13 15 17 19 PD/C 20 18 16 14 12 10 8 6 4 2

MR. BIGPERSON'S SIDE

Giants? I haven't seen giants in these parts since the old Queen's time.

Why shouldn't you listen to people
who have just come out of the moat?
Because they are all wet.

What is a kingdom?
A stupid king.

What knights ride camels?
The Arabian Nights.

What is the most dangerous
time for knights?
Nightfall.

Where did Sir John,
the giant killer, study?

In knight school.

What is a good sorcerer called?

A charming fellow.

What is a
nervous sorceress called?
A twitch.

Why do dragons sleep during the day?
So they can fight knights.

What is a knight's favorite fish?
A swordfish.

When a dragon is breathing fire,
how can you calm him down?
Throw water at him and he
will let off steam.

In those days you saw giants everywhere you turned.

Whole families of giants.

How do you tell a dinosaur to hurry up?
Pronto, Saurus.

For how long did Cain hate his brother?
As long as he was Abel.

How can you measure the depth of a giant's love?
By his sighs.

There is a family of giants with ten brothers. Each brother has a sister. How many children are there in the giant family?
Eleven.

Why did the giant name both of his sons Ed?
Because two Eds are better than one.

How do little fish make a living?
They start on a very small scale.

When a baby camel was born with no humps, what did his parents name him?
Humphrey.

What is a minimum?
A small mother.

Why did the giant name her first daughter Margarine?
Because she didn't have any but her.

They caused a lot of trouble.

What did the big toe say to the little toes?
There's a big heel following us.

What did the big shoe say to the little shoe?
You'll do in a pinch.

What is the difference between an oak tree and a tight shoe?
One makes acorns and the other makes corns ache.

What is 8 inches long and 3 inches wide, yet holds a whole foot?
A shoe.

Why is a giant's shoe like a generous person?
Because it has a large sole.

What do you have when you don't feel well?
You have gloves on your hands.

What steps should you take when you first see a giant?
Giant steps.

Why are a giant's fingers 11 inches long?
If they were an inch longer each finger would be a foot.

When shouldn't you hit a 10-inch nail with a hammer?
When it's on a giant's toe.

You could be sitting on the porch looking at the view...

**What sentence would you get
if you broke the law of gravity?**
A suspended sentence.

What did one angel say to the other?
Halo.

What did the little planet say when it broke out of orbit?
Look Mom, no gravities.

Where do snowflakes dance?
At a snowball.

**What is very light but
can't be lifted by the strongest giant?**
A bubble.

What is weathor?
A bad spell of weather.

Why does almost everyone enjoy astronomy?
Because it is heavenly.

What goes down but can never come up?
A well.

If a giant fell downstairs, what would he fall against?
Against his wishes.

Why can't a very thin giant stand up straight?
Because she is lean.

What constellation is like a naked giant?
The Great Bear.

and suddenly you'd be all socked in.

If you saw a giant waking up from a nap, what time would it be?
Time to run.

What question can a giant never answer "yes"?
Are you asleep?

What can overpower a giant without hurting him?
Sleep.

What will happen if you eat yeast and shoe polish?
You will rise and shine.

What has a soft bed but never sleeps, a big mouth but never speaks?
A river.

What friends should giants have around when they are very tired?
Nodding acquaintances.

Why did the giant tie a tiger, a lion, and an alligator to the foot of her bed?
She liked a few bites before going to sleep.

How do you know that giants are lazier than humans?
Because they lie longer in bed.

In the morning there would be a river running by the front door...

Which hand do giants use to stir their stew?
Neither, they use a spoon.

What happened to Ray when he was eaten by a giant?
He became X-Ray.

Why should you always stay calm when you meet a human-eating giant?
It's best not to get into a stew.

Why did the baby giant get punished for chasing the giant killer?
She wasn't supposed to play with her food.

How many 6-foot 6-inch men can a 66-foot giant eat on an empty stomach?
One. After that his stomach wouldn't be empty.

What is the difference between a hungry giant and a greedy giant?
One longs to eat and the other eats too long.

When do you see acrobats in the dining room?
When there are water tumblers on the table.

and in the afternoon there wouldn't be.

How did the big mountain know the little mountain was a liar?
Because it was only a bluff.

What did the big saltcellar say to the little saltcellar?
Let's shake.

Bigger than a giant, lighter than a feather. What is it?
The shadow of a giant.

What did the big raindrop say to the little raindrop?
My plop is bigger than your plop.

What did the big candle say to the little candle?
You're pretty bright for a little fellow.

What did the little hand say to the big hand?
I'll be back in an hour.

What did the big hand say to the little hand?
Got a minute?

What did the little magnet say to the big magnet?
I find you very attractive.

What is a foreign ant?
Important.

What ants are the biggest?

Giants.

Some giants messed up the weather.

Why did the giant watch the lazy cows?
She liked to see the meat loaf.

Why did the tractor hate the giant?
Because it couldn't bear him.

Why did the giant give sugar to his sick pig?
He wanted sugar-cured ham.

Why did the giant take a hammer to bed?
So that he could hit the hay.

What is a groundhog?
A big sausage.

What is a pharmacist?
A pharmer's helper.

What could the little giant push in a wheelbarrow that the big giant could not?
The big giant.

On what side of a giant's house does the beanstalk grow?
On the outside.

Where do little ears of corn come from?
The stalk brings them.

Why should you never tell secrets on the farm?
Because of the beanstalk there.

Some giants spoiled picnics.

Why are handcuffs like souvenirs?
They are made for two wrists.

Why does the Statue of Liberty stand in New York harbor?
Because it can't sit down.

How can you fall from the Empire State Building and not get hurt?
Fall from the front doorstep.

How have jets changed the world?
They have made it go plane crazy.

What should you do to stop from getting sick the night before a trip?
Leave a day earlier.

When is a giant not a giant?
When he's a little cross.

What does a cruise ship, completely loaded with giants, weigh when it leaves shore?
It weighs anchor.

What kind of crew does a ghost ship have?
A skeleton crew.

What puts the white lines on the ocean?
Ocean liners.

What makes the Leaning Tower of Pisa lean?
It never gets anything to eat.

Some giants were just plain mean.

If you were condemned to die,
what manner of death would you choose?
Old age.

A captured giant was chained to a 50-foot chain,
yet he walked 100 feet. How?
The chain wasn't attached to anything but the giant.

What is the largest room in the world?
Room for improvement.

Can you make one word from nine thumps?
Punishment.

Can two people stand 2 inches apart
without being able to touch each other?
Yes, just shut the door between them.

What did one drop of ink ask the other drop of ink?
Are all your relatives in the pen too?

What do you call someone who steals pigs?
A hamburgler.

Who doesn't mind being interrupted
in the middle of a sentence?
A convict.

Why is a thief always relaxed?
Because he takes things easy.

Why was Goliath surprised when David hit him with a stone?
Because such a thing had never entered his head before.

When must a giant keep his word?
When no one else will take it.

Ruffins

The baby giants were a special problem.

How do you spell blind giant? Blnd gant. You spell it that way because a blind giant has no eyes.

Which is easier to spell, fiddle-de-dee or fiddle-de-dum? Fiddle-de-dee is spelled with more E's.

Can you spell WE in two letters without using W or E? U and I.

What kind of jokes does a giant scholar make? Wisecracks.

Where does satisfaction come from? From a satisfactory.

What kind of paper can you tear? Terrible paper.

What liquid can't freeze? Boiling water.

What letter is a large body of water? C.

Where does eleven plus two equal one? ON A WATCH FACE.

There sure were giants in those days.

And big giants, too.

But I never see any giants now.

I don't think there are giants anymore.

Its A Kristopher